You are worthy.

Believe in

yourself

Acknowledging the good that you have in your life is the foundation for all

abundance

BENEFITS OF JOURNALING

- BOOSTS MOOD AND ENERGY
- BUILDS SELF ESTEEM
- IMPROVES MENTAL HEALTH
- REDUCES STRESS
- INSPIRES CREATIVITY
- ENHANCES RELATIONSHIPS

AND MUCH MORE...

GRATITUDE JOURNAL

DATE

S M T W T F S

I AM CAPABLE, STRONG, AND READY TO TAKE ON THE DAY.

THINGS I'M GRATEFUL FOR

1

2

3

THINGS THAT MADE ME SMILE TODAY

SOMETHING THAT INSPIRED ME TODAY

PEOPLE I'M GRATEFUL TO HAVE IN MY LIFE

Daily Affirmation

NOTES & FREE THOUGHTS

GRATITUDE JOURNAL

DATE

S M T W T F S

TODAY, I CHOOSE JOY, PEACE, AND POSITIVITY IN ALL I DO.

THINGS I'M GRATEFUL FOR

1

2

3

THINGS THAT MADE ME SMILE TODAY

SOMETHING THAT INSPIRED ME TODAY

PEOPLE I'M GRATEFUL TO HAVE IN MY LIFE

Daily Affirmation

NOTES & FREE THOUGHTS

GRATITUDE JOURNAL

DATE

S M T W T F S

I RADIATE CONFIDENCE, LOVE, AND KINDNESS IN ALL INTERACTIONS.

THINGS I'M GRATEFUL FOR

1

2

3

THINGS THAT MADE ME SMILE TODAY

SOMETHING THAT INSPIRED ME TODAY

PEOPLE I'M GRATEFUL TO HAVE IN MY LIFE

Daily Affirmation

NOTES & FREE THOUGHTS

GRATITUDE JOURNAL

DATE

S M T W T F S

I AM IN CONTROL OF MY THOUGHTS, EMOTIONS, AND ACTIONS TODAY.

THINGS I'M GRATEFUL FOR

1

2

3

THINGS THAT MADE ME SMILE TODAY

SOMETHING THAT INSPIRED ME TODAY

PEOPLE I'M GRATEFUL TO HAVE IN MY LIFE

Daily Affirmation

NOTES & FREE THOUGHTS

GRATITUDE JOURNAL

DATE

S M T W T F S

I HAVE EVERYTHING I NEED TO SUCCEED WITHIN ME.

THINGS I'M GRATEFUL FOR

1

2

3

THINGS THAT MADE ME SMILE TODAY

SOMETHING THAT INSPIRED ME TODAY

PEOPLE I'M GRATEFUL TO HAVE IN MY LIFE

Daily Affirmation

NOTES & FREE THOUGHTS

GRATITUDE JOURNAL

DATE

S M T W T F S

I WELCOME POSITIVITY INTO MY LIFE TODAY AND ALWAYS.

THINGS I'M GRATEFUL FOR

1

2

3

THINGS THAT MADE ME SMILE TODAY

SOMETHING THAT INSPIRED ME TODAY

PEOPLE I'M GRATEFUL TO HAVE IN MY LIFE

Daily Affirmation

NOTES & FREE THOUGHTS

GRATITUDE JOURNAL

DATE

S M T W T F S

MY MIND IS CLEAR, MY HEART IS OPEN, AND I AM READY TO EMBRACE THE DAY.

THINGS I'M GRATEFUL FOR

1

2

3

THINGS THAT MADE ME SMILE TODAY

SOMETHING THAT INSPIRED ME TODAY

PEOPLE I'M GRATEFUL TO HAVE IN MY LIFE

Daily Affirmation

NOTES & FREE THOUGHTS

Weekly check in

DATE

TOP 3 THINGS I DID THIS WEEK

- ○
- ○
- ○

MOST REWARDING INTERACTION I HAD THIS WEEK

THIS WEEK I FELT

NEXT WEEK I WANT TO

THINGS I ACCOMPLISHED THIS WEEK

WHAT WAS THE BEST THING ABOUT THE WEEK?

MY RANKING OF THE WEEK

☆ ☆ ☆ ☆ ☆

GRATITUDE JOURNAL

DATE

S M T W T F S

I AM CAPABLE, STRONG, AND READY TO TAKE ON THE DAY.

THINGS I'M GRATEFUL FOR

1

2

3

THINGS THAT MADE ME SMILE TODAY

SOMETHING THAT INSPIRED ME TODAY

PEOPLE I'M GRATEFUL TO HAVE IN MY LIFE

Daily Affirmation

NOTES & FREE THOUGHTS

GRATITUDE JOURNAL

DATE

S M T W T F S

I AM CAPABLE, STRONG, AND READY TO TAKE ON THE DAY.

THINGS I'M GRATEFUL FOR

1

2

3

THINGS THAT MADE ME SMILE TODAY

SOMETHING THAT INSPIRED ME TODAY

PEOPLE I'M GRATEFUL TO HAVE IN MY LIFE

Daily Affirmation

NOTES & FREE THOUGHTS

GRATITUDE JOURNAL

DATE

S M T W T F S

I AM CAPABLE, STRONG, AND READY TO TAKE ON THE DAY.

THINGS I'M GRATEFUL FOR

1

2

3

THINGS THAT MADE ME SMILE TODAY

SOMETHING THAT INSPIRED ME TODAY

PEOPLE I'M GRATEFUL TO HAVE IN MY LIFE

Daily Affirmation

NOTES & FREE THOUGHTS

GRATITUDE JOURNAL

DATE

S M T W T F S

TODAY, I CHOOSE JOY, PEACE, AND POSITIVITY IN ALL I DO.

THINGS I'M GRATEFUL FOR

1

2

3

THINGS THAT MADE ME SMILE TODAY

SOMETHING THAT INSPIRED ME TODAY

PEOPLE I'M GRATEFUL TO HAVE IN MY LIFE

Daily Affirmation

NOTES & FREE THOUGHTS

GRATITUDE JOURNAL

DATE

S M T W T F S

I RADIATE CONFIDENCE, LOVE, AND KINDNESS IN ALL INTERACTIONS.

THINGS I'M GRATEFUL FOR

1

2

3

THINGS THAT MADE ME SMILE TODAY

SOMETHING THAT INSPIRED ME TODAY

PEOPLE I'M GRATEFUL TO HAVE IN MY LIFE

Daily Affirmation

NOTES & FREE THOUGHTS

GRATITUDE JOURNAL

DATE

S M T W T F S

I AM IN CONTROL OF MY THOUGHTS, EMOTIONS, AND ACTIONS TODAY.

THINGS I'M GRATEFUL FOR

1

2

3

THINGS THAT MADE ME SMILE TODAY

SOMETHING THAT INSPIRED ME TODAY

PEOPLE I'M GRATEFUL TO HAVE IN MY LIFE

Daily Affirmation

NOTES & FREE THOUGHTS

GRATITUDE JOURNAL

DATE

S M T W T F S

I HAVE EVERYTHING I NEED TO SUCCEED WITHIN ME.

THINGS I'M GRATEFUL FOR

1

2

3

THINGS THAT MADE ME SMILE TODAY

SOMETHING THAT INSPIRED ME TODAY

PEOPLE I'M GRATEFUL TO HAVE IN MY LIFE

Daily Affirmation

NOTES & FREE THOUGHTS

GRATITUDE JOURNAL

DATE

S M T W T F S

I WELCOME POSITIVITY INTO MY LIFE TODAY AND ALWAYS.

THINGS I'M GRATEFUL FOR

1

2

3

THINGS THAT MADE ME SMILE TODAY

SOMETHING THAT INSPIRED ME TODAY

PEOPLE I'M GRATEFUL TO HAVE IN MY LIFE

Daily Affirmation

NOTES & FREE THOUGHTS

GRATITUDE JOURNAL

DATE

S M T W T F S

MY MIND IS CLEAR, MY HEART IS OPEN, AND I AM READY TO EMBRACE THE DAY.

THINGS I'M GRATEFUL FOR

1

2

3

THINGS THAT MADE ME SMILE TODAY

SOMETHING THAT INSPIRED ME TODAY

PEOPLE I'M GRATEFUL TO HAVE IN MY LIFE

Daily Affirmation

NOTES & FREE THOUGHTS

Weekly check in

DATE

TOP 3 THINGS I DID THIS WEEK

- ○
- ○
- ○

MOST REWARDING INTERACTION I HAD THIS WEEK

THIS WEEK I FELT

NEXT WEEK I WANT TO

THINGS I ACCOMPLISHED THIS WEEK

WHAT WAS THE BEST THING ABOUT THE WEEK?

MY RANKING OF THE WEEK

☆ ☆ ☆ ☆ ☆

GRATITUDE JOURNAL

DATE

S M T W T F S

TODAY, I CHOOSE JOY, PEACE, AND POSITIVITY IN ALL I DO.

THINGS I'M GRATEFUL FOR

1

2

3

THINGS THAT MADE ME SMILE TODAY

SOMETHING THAT INSPIRED ME TODAY

PEOPLE I'M GRATEFUL TO HAVE IN MY LIFE

Daily Affirmation

NOTES & FREE THOUGHTS

GRATITUDE JOURNAL

DATE

S M T W T F S

I RADIATE CONFIDENCE, LOVE, AND KINDNESS IN ALL INTERACTIONS.

THINGS I'M GRATEFUL FOR

1

2

3

THINGS THAT MADE ME SMILE TODAY

SOMETHING THAT INSPIRED ME TODAY

PEOPLE I'M GRATEFUL TO HAVE IN MY LIFE

Daily Affirmation

NOTES & FREE THOUGHTS

GRATITUDE JOURNAL

DATE

S M T W T F S

I AM IN CONTROL OF MY THOUGHTS, EMOTIONS, AND ACTIONS TODAY.

THINGS I'M GRATEFUL FOR

1

2

3

THINGS THAT MADE ME SMILE TODAY

SOMETHING THAT INSPIRED ME TODAY

PEOPLE I'M GRATEFUL TO HAVE IN MY LIFE

Daily Affirmation

NOTES & FREE THOUGHTS

GRATITUDE JOURNAL

DATE

S M T W T F S

I HAVE EVERYTHING I NEED TO SUCCEED WITHIN ME.

THINGS I'M GRATEFUL FOR

1

2

3

THINGS THAT MADE ME SMILE TODAY

SOMETHING THAT INSPIRED ME TODAY

PEOPLE I'M GRATEFUL TO HAVE IN MY LIFE

Daily Affirmation

NOTES & FREE THOUGHTS

GRATITUDE JOURNAL

DATE

S M T W T F S

I WELCOME POSITIVITY INTO MY LIFE TODAY AND ALWAYS.

THINGS I'M GRATEFUL FOR

1

2

3

THINGS THAT MADE ME SMILE TODAY

SOMETHING THAT INSPIRED ME TODAY

PEOPLE I'M GRATEFUL TO HAVE IN MY LIFE

Daily Affirmation

NOTES & FREE THOUGHTS

GRATITUDE JOURNAL

DATE

S M T W T F S

MY MIND IS CLEAR, MY HEART IS OPEN, AND I AM READY TO EMBRACE THE DAY.

THINGS I'M GRATEFUL FOR

1

2

3

THINGS THAT MADE ME SMILE TODAY

SOMETHING THAT INSPIRED ME TODAY

PEOPLE I'M GRATEFUL TO HAVE IN MY LIFE

Daily Affirmation

NOTES & FREE THOUGHTS

Weekly check in

DATE

TOP 3 THINGS I DID THIS WEEK

○

○

○

MOST REWARDING INTERACTION I HAD THIS WEEK

THIS WEEK I FELT

NEXT WEEK I WANT TO

THINGS I ACCOMPLISHED THIS WEEK

WHAT WAS THE BEST THING ABOUT THE WEEK?

MY RANKING OF THE WEEK

GRATITUDE JOURNAL

DATE

S M T W T F S

TODAY, I CHOOSE JOY, PEACE, AND POSITIVITY IN ALL I DO.

THINGS I'M GRATEFUL FOR

1

2

3

THINGS THAT MADE ME SMILE TODAY

SOMETHING THAT INSPIRED ME TODAY

PEOPLE I'M GRATEFUL TO HAVE IN MY LIFE

Daily Affirmation

NOTES & FREE THOUGHTS

GRATITUDE JOURNAL

DATE

S M T W T F S

I RADIATE CONFIDENCE, LOVE, AND KINDNESS IN ALL INTERACTIONS.

THINGS I'M GRATEFUL FOR

1

2

3

THINGS THAT MADE ME SMILE TODAY

SOMETHING THAT INSPIRED ME TODAY

PEOPLE I'M GRATEFUL TO HAVE IN MY LIFE

Daily Affirmation

NOTES & FREE THOUGHTS

GRATITUDE JOURNAL

DATE

S M T W T F S

I AM IN CONTROL OF MY THOUGHTS, EMOTIONS, AND ACTIONS TODAY.

THINGS I'M GRATEFUL FOR

1

2

3

THINGS THAT MADE ME SMILE TODAY

SOMETHING THAT INSPIRED ME TODAY

PEOPLE I'M GRATEFUL TO HAVE IN MY LIFE

Daily Affirmation

NOTES & FREE THOUGHTS

GRATITUDE JOURNAL

DATE

S M T W T F S

I HAVE EVERYTHING I NEED TO SUCCEED WITHIN ME.

THINGS I'M GRATEFUL FOR

1

2

3

THINGS THAT MADE ME SMILE TODAY

SOMETHING THAT INSPIRED ME TODAY

PEOPLE I'M GRATEFUL TO HAVE IN MY LIFE

Daily Affirmation

NOTES & FREE THOUGHTS

GRATITUDE JOURNAL

DATE

S M T W T F S

I WELCOME POSITIVITY INTO MY LIFE TODAY AND ALWAYS.

THINGS I'M GRATEFUL FOR

1

2

3

THINGS THAT MADE ME SMILE TODAY

SOMETHING THAT INSPIRED ME TODAY

PEOPLE I'M GRATEFUL TO HAVE IN MY LIFE

Daily Affirmation

NOTES & FREE THOUGHTS

GRATITUDE JOURNAL

DATE

S M T W T F S

MY MIND IS CLEAR, MY HEART IS OPEN, AND I AM READY TO EMBRACE THE DAY.

THINGS I'M GRATEFUL FOR

1

2

3

THINGS THAT MADE ME SMILE TODAY

SOMETHING THAT INSPIRED ME TODAY

PEOPLE I'M GRATEFUL TO HAVE IN MY LIFE

Daily Affirmation

NOTES & FREE THOUGHTS

Weekly check in

DATE

TOP 3 THINGS I DID THIS WEEK

- ○
- ○
- ○

MOST REWARDING INTERACTION I HAD THIS WEEK

THIS WEEK I FELT

NEXT WEEK I WANT TO

THINGS I ACCOMPLISHED THIS WEEK

WHAT WAS THE BEST THING ABOUT THE WEEK?

MY RANKING OF THE WEEK

☆ ☆ ☆ ☆ ☆

People / Places / Experience that filled your heart with love and joy in the last few weeks

GRATITUDE JOURNAL

DATE

S M T W T F S

I AM CAPABLE, STRONG, AND READY TO TAKE ON THE DAY.

THINGS I'M GRATEFUL FOR

1

2

3

THINGS THAT MADE ME SMILE TODAY

SOMETHING THAT INSPIRED ME TODAY

PEOPLE I'M GRATEFUL TO HAVE IN MY LIFE

Daily Affirmation

NOTES & FREE THOUGHTS

GRATITUDE JOURNAL

DATE

S M T W T F S

TODAY, I CHOOSE JOY, PEACE, AND POSITIVITY IN ALL I DO.

THINGS I'M GRATEFUL FOR

1

2

3

THINGS THAT MADE ME SMILE TODAY

SOMETHING THAT INSPIRED ME TODAY

PEOPLE I'M GRATEFUL TO HAVE IN MY LIFE

Daily Affirmation

NOTES & FREE THOUGHTS

GRATITUDE JOURNAL

DATE

S M T W T F S

I RADIATE CONFIDENCE, LOVE, AND KINDNESS IN ALL INTERACTIONS.

THINGS I'M GRATEFUL FOR

1

2

3

THINGS THAT MADE ME SMILE TODAY

SOMETHING THAT INSPIRED ME TODAY

PEOPLE I'M GRATEFUL TO HAVE IN MY LIFE

Daily Affirmation

NOTES & FREE THOUGHTS

GRATITUDE JOURNAL

DATE

S M T W T F S

I AM IN CONTROL OF MY THOUGHTS, EMOTIONS, AND ACTIONS TODAY.

THINGS I'M GRATEFUL FOR

1

2

3

THINGS THAT MADE ME SMILE TODAY

SOMETHING THAT INSPIRED ME TODAY

PEOPLE I'M GRATEFUL TO HAVE IN MY LIFE

Daily Affirmation

NOTES & FREE THOUGHTS

GRATITUDE JOURNAL

DATE

S M T W T F S

I HAVE EVERYTHING I NEED TO SUCCEED WITHIN ME.

THINGS I'M GRATEFUL FOR

1

2

3

THINGS THAT MADE ME SMILE TODAY

SOMETHING THAT INSPIRED ME TODAY

PEOPLE I'M GRATEFUL TO HAVE IN MY LIFE

Daily Affirmation

NOTES & FREE THOUGHTS

GRATITUDE JOURNAL

DATE

S M T W T F S

I WELCOME POSITIVITY INTO MY LIFE TODAY AND ALWAYS.

THINGS I'M GRATEFUL FOR

1

2

3

THINGS THAT MADE ME SMILE TODAY

SOMETHING THAT INSPIRED ME TODAY

PEOPLE I'M GRATEFUL TO HAVE IN MY LIFE

Daily Affirmation

NOTES & FREE THOUGHTS

GRATITUDE JOURNAL

DATE

S M T W T F S

MY MIND IS CLEAR, MY HEART IS OPEN, AND I AM READY TO EMBRACE THE DAY.

THINGS I'M GRATEFUL FOR

1

2

3

THINGS THAT MADE ME SMILE TODAY

SOMETHING THAT INSPIRED ME TODAY

PEOPLE I'M GRATEFUL TO HAVE IN MY LIFE

Daily Affirmation

NOTES & FREE THOUGHTS

Weekly check in

DATE

TOP 3 THINGS I DID THIS WEEK

○

○

○

MOST REWARDING INTERACTION I HAD THIS WEEK

THIS WEEK I FELT

NEXT WEEK I WANT TO

THINGS I ACCOMPLISHED THIS WEEK

WHAT WAS THE BEST THING ABOUT THE WEEK?

MY RANKING OF THE WEEK

GRATITUDE JOURNAL

DATE

S M T W T F S

I AM CAPABLE, STRONG, AND READY TO TAKE ON THE DAY.

THINGS I'M GRATEFUL FOR

1

2

3

THINGS THAT MADE ME SMILE TODAY

SOMETHING THAT INSPIRED ME TODAY

PEOPLE I'M GRATEFUL TO HAVE IN MY LIFE

Daily Affirmation

NOTES & FREE THOUGHTS

GRATITUDE JOURNAL

DATE

S M T W T F S

TODAY, I CHOOSE JOY, PEACE, AND POSITIVITY IN ALL I DO.

THINGS I'M GRATEFUL FOR

1

2

3

THINGS THAT MADE ME SMILE TODAY

SOMETHING THAT INSPIRED ME TODAY

PEOPLE I'M GRATEFUL TO HAVE IN MY LIFE

Daily Affirmation

NOTES & FREE THOUGHTS

GRATITUDE JOURNAL

DATE

S M T W T F S

I RADIATE CONFIDENCE, LOVE, AND KINDNESS IN ALL INTERACTIONS.

THINGS I'M GRATEFUL FOR

1

2

3

THINGS THAT MADE ME SMILE TODAY

SOMETHING THAT INSPIRED ME TODAY

PEOPLE I'M GRATEFUL TO HAVE IN MY LIFE

Daily Affirmation

NOTES & FREE THOUGHTS

GRATITUDE JOURNAL

DATE

S M T W T F S

I AM IN CONTROL OF MY THOUGHTS, EMOTIONS, AND ACTIONS TODAY.

THINGS I'M GRATEFUL FOR

1

2

3

THINGS THAT MADE ME SMILE TODAY

SOMETHING THAT INSPIRED ME TODAY

PEOPLE I'M GRATEFUL TO HAVE IN MY LIFE

Daily Affirmation

NOTES & FREE THOUGHTS

GRATITUDE JOURNAL

DATE

S M T W T F S

I HAVE EVERYTHING I NEED TO SUCCEED WITHIN ME.

THINGS I'M GRATEFUL FOR

1

2

3

THINGS THAT MADE ME SMILE TODAY

SOMETHING THAT INSPIRED ME TODAY

PEOPLE I'M GRATEFUL TO HAVE IN MY LIFE

Daily Affirmation

NOTES & FREE THOUGHTS

GRATITUDE JOURNAL

DATE

S M T W T F S

I WELCOME POSITIVITY INTO MY LIFE TODAY AND ALWAYS.

THINGS I'M GRATEFUL FOR

1

2

3

THINGS THAT MADE ME SMILE TODAY

SOMETHING THAT INSPIRED ME TODAY

PEOPLE I'M GRATEFUL TO HAVE IN MY LIFE

Daily Affirmation

NOTES & FREE THOUGHTS

GRATITUDE JOURNAL

DATE

S M T W T F S

MY MIND IS CLEAR, MY HEART IS OPEN, AND I AM READY TO EMBRACE THE DAY.

THINGS I'M GRATEFUL FOR

1

2

3

THINGS THAT MADE ME SMILE TODAY

SOMETHING THAT INSPIRED ME TODAY

PEOPLE I'M GRATEFUL TO HAVE IN MY LIFE

Daily Affirmation

NOTES & FREE THOUGHTS

Weekly check in

DATE

TOP 3 THINGS I DID THIS WEEK

- ○
- ○
- ○

MOST REWARDING INTERACTION I HAD THIS WEEK

THIS WEEK I FELT

NEXT WEEK I WANT TO

THINGS I ACCOMPLISHED THIS WEEK

WHAT WAS THE BEST THING ABOUT THE WEEK?

MY RANKING OF THE WEEK

GRATITUDE JOURNAL

DATE

S M T W T F S

I AM CAPABLE, STRONG, AND READY TO TAKE ON THE DAY.

THINGS I'M GRATEFUL FOR

1

2

3

THINGS THAT MADE ME SMILE TODAY

SOMETHING THAT INSPIRED ME TODAY

PEOPLE I'M GRATEFUL TO HAVE IN MY LIFE

Daily Affirmation

NOTES & FREE THOUGHTS

GRATITUDE JOURNAL

DATE

S M T W T F S

TODAY, I CHOOSE JOY, PEACE, AND POSITIVITY IN ALL I DO.

THINGS I'M GRATEFUL FOR

1

2

3

THINGS THAT MADE ME SMILE TODAY

SOMETHING THAT INSPIRED ME TODAY

PEOPLE I'M GRATEFUL TO HAVE IN MY LIFE

Daily Affirmation

NOTES & FREE THOUGHTS

GRATITUDE JOURNAL

DATE

S M T W T F S

I RADIATE CONFIDENCE, LOVE, AND KINDNESS IN ALL INTERACTIONS.

THINGS I'M GRATEFUL FOR

1

2

3

THINGS THAT MADE ME SMILE TODAY

SOMETHING THAT INSPIRED ME TODAY

PEOPLE I'M GRATEFUL TO HAVE IN MY LIFE

Daily Affirmation

NOTES & FREE THOUGHTS

GRATITUDE JOURNAL

DATE

S M T W T F S

I AM IN CONTROL OF MY THOUGHTS, EMOTIONS, AND ACTIONS TODAY.

THINGS I'M GRATEFUL FOR

1

2

3

THINGS THAT MADE ME SMILE TODAY

SOMETHING THAT INSPIRED ME TODAY

PEOPLE I'M GRATEFUL TO HAVE IN MY LIFE

Daily Affirmation

NOTES & FREE THOUGHTS

GRATITUDE JOURNAL

DATE

S M T W T F S

I HAVE EVERYTHING I NEED TO SUCCEED WITHIN ME.

THINGS I'M GRATEFUL FOR

1

2

3

THINGS THAT MADE ME SMILE TODAY

SOMETHING THAT INSPIRED ME TODAY

PEOPLE I'M GRATEFUL TO HAVE IN MY LIFE

Daily Affirmation

NOTES & FREE THOUGHTS

GRATITUDE JOURNAL

DATE

S M T W T F S

I WELCOME POSITIVITY INTO MY LIFE TODAY AND ALWAYS.

THINGS I'M GRATEFUL FOR

1

2

3

THINGS THAT MADE ME SMILE TODAY

SOMETHING THAT INSPIRED ME TODAY

PEOPLE I'M GRATEFUL TO HAVE IN MY LIFE

Daily Affirmation

NOTES & FREE THOUGHTS

GRATITUDE JOURNAL

DATE

S M T W T F S

MY MIND IS CLEAR, MY HEART IS OPEN, AND I AM READY TO EMBRACE THE DAY.

THINGS I'M GRATEFUL FOR

1

2

3

THINGS THAT MADE ME SMILE TODAY

SOMETHING THAT INSPIRED ME TODAY

PEOPLE I'M GRATEFUL TO HAVE IN MY LIFE

Daily Affirmation

NOTES & FREE THOUGHTS

Weekly check in

DATE

TOP 3 THINGS I DID THIS WEEK

- ○
- ○
- ○

MOST REWARDING INTERACTION I HAD THIS WEEK

THIS WEEK I FELT

NEXT WEEK I WANT TO

THINGS I ACCOMPLISHED THIS WEEK

WHAT WAS THE BEST THING ABOUT THE WEEK?

MY RANKING OF THE WEEK

GRATITUDE JOURNAL

DATE

S M T W T F S

I AM CAPABLE, STRONG, AND READY TO TAKE ON THE DAY.

THINGS I'M GRATEFUL FOR

1

2

3

THINGS THAT MADE ME SMILE TODAY

SOMETHING THAT INSPIRED ME TODAY

PEOPLE I'M GRATEFUL TO HAVE IN MY LIFE

Daily Affirmation

NOTES & FREE THOUGHTS

GRATITUDE JOURNAL

DATE

S M T W T F S

TODAY, I CHOOSE JOY, PEACE, AND POSITIVITY IN ALL I DO.

THINGS I'M GRATEFUL FOR

1

2

3

THINGS THAT MADE ME SMILE TODAY

SOMETHING THAT INSPIRED ME TODAY

PEOPLE I'M GRATEFUL TO HAVE IN MY LIFE

Daily Affirmation

NOTES & FREE THOUGHTS

GRATITUDE JOURNAL

DATE

S M T W T F S

I RADIATE CONFIDENCE, LOVE, AND KINDNESS IN ALL INTERACTIONS.

THINGS I'M GRATEFUL FOR

1

2

3

THINGS THAT MADE ME SMILE TODAY

SOMETHING THAT INSPIRED ME TODAY

PEOPLE I'M GRATEFUL TO HAVE IN MY LIFE

Daily Affirmation

NOTES & FREE THOUGHTS

GRATITUDE JOURNAL

DATE

S M T W T F S

I AM IN CONTROL OF MY THOUGHTS, EMOTIONS, AND ACTIONS TODAY.

THINGS I'M GRATEFUL FOR

1

2

3

THINGS THAT MADE ME SMILE TODAY

SOMETHING THAT INSPIRED ME TODAY

PEOPLE I'M GRATEFUL TO HAVE IN MY LIFE

Daily Affirmation

NOTES & FREE THOUGHTS

GRATITUDE JOURNAL

DATE

S M T W T F S

I HAVE EVERYTHING I NEED TO SUCCEED WITHIN ME.

THINGS I'M GRATEFUL FOR

1

2

3

THINGS THAT MADE ME SMILE TODAY

SOMETHING THAT INSPIRED ME TODAY

PEOPLE I'M GRATEFUL TO HAVE IN MY LIFE

Daily Affirmation

NOTES & FREE THOUGHTS

GRATITUDE JOURNAL

DATE

S M T W T F S

I WELCOME POSITIVITY INTO MY LIFE TODAY AND ALWAYS.

THINGS I'M GRATEFUL FOR

1

2

3

THINGS THAT MADE ME SMILE TODAY

SOMETHING THAT INSPIRED ME TODAY

PEOPLE I'M GRATEFUL TO HAVE IN MY LIFE

Daily Affirmation

NOTES & FREE THOUGHTS

GRATITUDE JOURNAL

DATE

S M T W T F S

MY MIND IS CLEAR, MY HEART IS OPEN, AND I AM READY TO EMBRACE THE DAY.

THINGS I'M GRATEFUL FOR

1

2

3

THINGS THAT MADE ME SMILE TODAY

SOMETHING THAT INSPIRED ME TODAY

PEOPLE I'M GRATEFUL TO HAVE IN MY LIFE

Daily Affirmation

NOTES & FREE THOUGHTS

Weekly check in

DATE

TOP 3 THINGS I DID THIS WEEK

- ○
- ○
- ○

MOST REWARDING INTERACTION I HAD THIS WEEK

THIS WEEK I FELT

NEXT WEEK I WANT TO

THINGS I ACCOMPLISHED THIS WEEK

WHAT WAS THE BEST THING ABOUT THE WEEK?

MY RANKING OF THE WEEK

People / Places / Experience that filled your heart with love and joy in the last few weeks

GRATITUDE JOURNAL

DATE

S M T W T F S

I AM CAPABLE, STRONG, AND READY TO TAKE ON THE DAY.

THINGS I'M GRATEFUL FOR

1

2

3

THINGS THAT MADE ME SMILE TODAY

SOMETHING THAT INSPIRED ME TODAY

PEOPLE I'M GRATEFUL TO HAVE IN MY LIFE

Daily Affirmation

NOTES & FREE THOUGHTS

GRATITUDE JOURNAL

DATE

S M T W T F S

TODAY, I CHOOSE JOY, PEACE, AND POSITIVITY IN ALL I DO.

THINGS I'M GRATEFUL FOR

1

2

3

THINGS THAT MADE ME SMILE TODAY

SOMETHING THAT INSPIRED ME TODAY

PEOPLE I'M GRATEFUL TO HAVE IN MY LIFE

Daily Affirmation

NOTES & FREE THOUGHTS

GRATITUDE JOURNAL

DATE

S M T W T F S

I AM CAPABLE, STRONG, AND READY TO TAKE ON THE DAY.

THINGS I'M GRATEFUL FOR

1

2

3

THINGS THAT MADE ME SMILE TODAY

SOMETHING THAT INSPIRED ME TODAY

PEOPLE I'M GRATEFUL TO HAVE IN MY LIFE

Daily Affirmation

NOTES & FREE THOUGHTS

GRATITUDE JOURNAL

DATE

S M T W T F S

TODAY, I CHOOSE JOY, PEACE, AND POSITIVITY IN ALL I DO.

THINGS I'M GRATEFUL FOR

1

2

3

THINGS THAT MADE ME SMILE TODAY

SOMETHING THAT INSPIRED ME TODAY

PEOPLE I'M GRATEFUL TO HAVE IN MY LIFE

Daily Affirmation

NOTES & FREE THOUGHTS

GRATITUDE JOURNAL

DATE

S M T W T F S

I RADIATE CONFIDENCE, LOVE, AND KINDNESS IN ALL INTERACTIONS.

THINGS I'M GRATEFUL FOR

1

2

3

THINGS THAT MADE ME SMILE TODAY

SOMETHING THAT INSPIRED ME TODAY

PEOPLE I'M GRATEFUL TO HAVE IN MY LIFE

Daily Affirmation

NOTES & FREE THOUGHTS

GRATITUDE JOURNAL

DATE

S M T W T F S

I AM IN CONTROL OF MY THOUGHTS, EMOTIONS, AND ACTIONS TODAY.

THINGS I'M GRATEFUL FOR

1

2

3

THINGS THAT MADE ME SMILE TODAY

SOMETHING THAT INSPIRED ME TODAY

PEOPLE I'M GRATEFUL TO HAVE IN MY LIFE

Daily Affirmation

NOTES & FREE THOUGHTS

GRATITUDE JOURNAL

DATE

S M T W T F S

I HAVE EVERYTHING I NEED TO SUCCEED WITHIN ME.

THINGS I'M GRATEFUL FOR

1

2

3

THINGS THAT MADE ME SMILE TODAY

SOMETHING THAT INSPIRED ME TODAY

PEOPLE I'M GRATEFUL TO HAVE IN MY LIFE

Daily Affirmation

NOTES & FREE THOUGHTS

GRATITUDE JOURNAL

DATE

S M T W T F S

I WELCOME POSITIVITY INTO MY LIFE TODAY AND ALWAYS.

THINGS I'M GRATEFUL FOR

1

2

3

THINGS THAT MADE ME SMILE TODAY

SOMETHING THAT INSPIRED ME TODAY

PEOPLE I'M GRATEFUL TO HAVE IN MY LIFE

Daily Affirmation

NOTES & FREE THOUGHTS

GRATITUDE JOURNAL

DATE

S M T W T F S

MY MIND IS CLEAR, MY HEART IS OPEN, AND I AM READY TO EMBRACE THE DAY.

THINGS I'M GRATEFUL FOR

1

2

3

THINGS THAT MADE ME SMILE TODAY

SOMETHING THAT INSPIRED ME TODAY

PEOPLE I'M GRATEFUL TO HAVE IN MY LIFE

Daily Affirmation

NOTES & FREE THOUGHTS

Weekly check in

DATE

TOP 3 THINGS I DID THIS WEEK

○

○

○

THIS WEEK I FELT

NEXT WEEK I WANT TO

MOST REWARDING INTERACTION I HAD THIS WEEK

THINGS I ACCOMPLISHED THIS WEEK

WHAT WAS THE BEST THING ABOUT THE WEEK?

MY RANKING OF THE WEEK

☆ ☆ ☆ ☆ ☆

GRATITUDE JOURNAL

DATE

S M T W T F S

I AM CAPABLE, STRONG, AND READY TO TAKE ON THE DAY.

THINGS I'M GRATEFUL FOR

1

2

3

THINGS THAT MADE ME SMILE TODAY

SOMETHING THAT INSPIRED ME TODAY

PEOPLE I'M GRATEFUL TO HAVE IN MY LIFE

Daily Affirmation

NOTES & FREE THOUGHTS

GRATITUDE JOURNAL

DATE

S M T W T F S

TODAY, I CHOOSE JOY, PEACE, AND POSITIVITY IN ALL I DO.

THINGS I'M GRATEFUL FOR

1

2

3

THINGS THAT MADE ME SMILE TODAY

SOMETHING THAT INSPIRED ME TODAY

PEOPLE I'M GRATEFUL TO HAVE IN MY LIFE

Daily Affirmation

NOTES & FREE THOUGHTS

GRATITUDE JOURNAL

DATE

S M T W T F S

I RADIATE CONFIDENCE, LOVE, AND KINDNESS IN ALL INTERACTIONS.

THINGS I'M GRATEFUL FOR

1

2

3

THINGS THAT MADE ME SMILE TODAY

SOMETHING THAT INSPIRED ME TODAY

PEOPLE I'M GRATEFUL TO HAVE IN MY LIFE

Daily Affirmation

NOTES & FREE THOUGHTS

GRATITUDE JOURNAL

DATE

S M T W T F S

I AM IN CONTROL OF MY THOUGHTS, EMOTIONS, AND ACTIONS TODAY.

THINGS I'M GRATEFUL FOR

1

2

3

THINGS THAT MADE ME SMILE TODAY

SOMETHING THAT INSPIRED ME TODAY

PEOPLE I'M GRATEFUL TO HAVE IN MY LIFE

Daily Affirmation

NOTES & FREE THOUGHTS

GRATITUDE JOURNAL

DATE

S M T W T F S

I HAVE EVERYTHING I NEED TO SUCCEED WITHIN ME.

THINGS I'M GRATEFUL FOR

1

2

3

THINGS THAT MADE ME SMILE TODAY

SOMETHING THAT INSPIRED ME TODAY

PEOPLE I'M GRATEFUL TO HAVE IN MY LIFE

Daily Affirmation

NOTES & FREE THOUGHTS

GRATITUDE JOURNAL

DATE

S M T W T F S

I WELCOME POSITIVITY INTO MY LIFE TODAY AND ALWAYS.

THINGS I'M GRATEFUL FOR

1

2

3

THINGS THAT MADE ME SMILE TODAY

SOMETHING THAT INSPIRED ME TODAY

PEOPLE I'M GRATEFUL TO HAVE IN MY LIFE

Daily Affirmation

NOTES & FREE THOUGHTS

GRATITUDE JOURNAL

DATE

S M T W T F S

MY MIND IS CLEAR, MY HEART IS OPEN, AND I AM READY TO EMBRACE THE DAY.

THINGS I'M GRATEFUL FOR

1

2

3

THINGS THAT MADE ME SMILE TODAY

SOMETHING THAT INSPIRED ME TODAY

PEOPLE I'M GRATEFUL TO HAVE IN MY LIFE

Daily Affirmation

NOTES & FREE THOUGHTS

Weekly check in

DATE

TOP 3 THINGS I DID THIS WEEK

- ○
- ○
- ○

THIS WEEK I FELT

MOST REWARDING INTERACTION I HAD THIS WEEK

NEXT WEEK I WANT TO

THINGS I ACCOMPLISHED THIS WEEK

WHAT WAS THE BEST THING ABOUT THE WEEK?

MY RANKING OF THE WEEK

☆ ☆ ☆ ☆ ☆

GRATITUDE JOURNAL

DATE

S M T W T F S

I AM CAPABLE, STRONG, AND READY TO TAKE ON THE DAY.

THINGS I'M GRATEFUL FOR

1

2

3

THINGS THAT MADE ME SMILE TODAY

SOMETHING THAT INSPIRED ME TODAY

PEOPLE I'M GRATEFUL TO HAVE IN MY LIFE

Daily Affirmation

NOTES & FREE THOUGHTS

GRATITUDE JOURNAL

DATE

S M T W T F S

TODAY, I CHOOSE JOY, PEACE, AND POSITIVITY IN ALL I DO.

THINGS I'M GRATEFUL FOR

1

2

3

THINGS THAT MADE ME SMILE TODAY

SOMETHING THAT INSPIRED ME TODAY

PEOPLE I'M GRATEFUL TO HAVE IN MY LIFE

Daily Affirmation

NOTES & FREE THOUGHTS

GRATITUDE JOURNAL

DATE

S M T W T F S

I RADIATE CONFIDENCE, LOVE, AND KINDNESS IN ALL INTERACTIONS.

THINGS I'M GRATEFUL FOR

1

2

3

THINGS THAT MADE ME SMILE TODAY

SOMETHING THAT INSPIRED ME TODAY

PEOPLE I'M GRATEFUL TO HAVE IN MY LIFE

Daily Affirmation

NOTES & FREE THOUGHTS

GRATITUDE JOURNAL

DATE

S M T W T F S

I AM IN CONTROL OF MY THOUGHTS, EMOTIONS, AND ACTIONS TODAY.

THINGS I'M GRATEFUL FOR

1

2

3

THINGS THAT MADE ME SMILE TODAY

SOMETHING THAT INSPIRED ME TODAY

PEOPLE I'M GRATEFUL TO HAVE IN MY LIFE

Daily Affirmation

NOTES & FREE THOUGHTS

GRATITUDE JOURNAL

DATE

S M T W T F S

I HAVE EVERYTHING I NEED TO SUCCEED WITHIN ME.

THINGS I'M GRATEFUL FOR

1

2

3

THINGS THAT MADE ME SMILE TODAY

SOMETHING THAT INSPIRED ME TODAY

PEOPLE I'M GRATEFUL TO HAVE IN MY LIFE

Daily Affirmation

NOTES & FREE THOUGHTS

GRATITUDE JOURNAL

DATE

S M T W T F S

I WELCOME POSITIVITY INTO MY LIFE TODAY AND ALWAYS.

THINGS I'M GRATEFUL FOR

1

2

3

THINGS THAT MADE ME SMILE TODAY

SOMETHING THAT INSPIRED ME TODAY

PEOPLE I'M GRATEFUL TO HAVE IN MY LIFE

Daily Affirmation

NOTES & FREE THOUGHTS

GRATITUDE JOURNAL

DATE

S M T W T F S

MY MIND IS CLEAR, MY HEART IS OPEN, AND I AM READY TO EMBRACE THE DAY.

THINGS I'M GRATEFUL FOR

1

2

3

THINGS THAT MADE ME SMILE TODAY

SOMETHING THAT INSPIRED ME TODAY

PEOPLE I'M GRATEFUL TO HAVE IN MY LIFE

Daily Affirmation

NOTES & FREE THOUGHTS

Weekly check in

DATE

TOP 3 THINGS I DID THIS WEEK

- ○
- ○
- ○

MOST REWARDING INTERACTION I HAD THIS WEEK

THIS WEEK I FELT

NEXT WEEK I WANT TO

THINGS I ACCOMPLISHED THIS WEEK

WHAT WAS THE BEST THING ABOUT THE WEEK?

MY RANKING OF THE WEEK

☆ ☆ ☆ ☆ ☆

GRATITUDE JOURNAL

DATE

S M T W T F S

I RADIATE CONFIDENCE, LOVE, AND KINDNESS IN ALL INTERACTIONS.

THINGS I'M GRATEFUL FOR

1

2

3

THINGS THAT MADE ME SMILE TODAY

SOMETHING THAT INSPIRED ME TODAY

PEOPLE I'M GRATEFUL TO HAVE IN MY LIFE

Daily Affirmation

NOTES & FREE THOUGHTS

GRATITUDE JOURNAL

DATE

S M T W T F S

I AM IN CONTROL OF MY THOUGHTS, EMOTIONS, AND ACTIONS TODAY.

THINGS I'M GRATEFUL FOR

1

2

3

THINGS THAT MADE ME SMILE TODAY

SOMETHING THAT INSPIRED ME TODAY

PEOPLE I'M GRATEFUL TO HAVE IN MY LIFE

Daily Affirmation

NOTES & FREE THOUGHTS

GRATITUDE JOURNAL

DATE

S M T W T F S

I HAVE EVERYTHING I NEED TO SUCCEED WITHIN ME.

THINGS I'M GRATEFUL FOR

1

2

3

THINGS THAT MADE ME SMILE TODAY

SOMETHING THAT INSPIRED ME TODAY

PEOPLE I'M GRATEFUL TO HAVE IN MY LIFE

Daily Affirmation

NOTES & FREE THOUGHTS

GRATITUDE JOURNAL

DATE

S M T W T F S

I WELCOME POSITIVITY INTO MY LIFE TODAY AND ALWAYS.

THINGS I'M GRATEFUL FOR

1

2

3

THINGS THAT MADE ME SMILE TODAY

SOMETHING THAT INSPIRED ME TODAY

PEOPLE I'M GRATEFUL TO HAVE IN MY LIFE

Daily Affirmation

NOTES & FREE THOUGHTS

GRATITUDE JOURNAL

DATE

S M T W T F S

MY MIND IS CLEAR, MY HEART IS OPEN, AND I AM READY TO EMBRACE THE DAY.

THINGS I'M GRATEFUL FOR

1

2

3

THINGS THAT MADE ME SMILE TODAY

SOMETHING THAT INSPIRED ME TODAY

PEOPLE I'M GRATEFUL TO HAVE IN MY LIFE

Daily Affirmation

NOTES & FREE THOUGHTS

Weekly check in

DATE

TOP 3 THINGS I DID THIS WEEK

- ○
- ○
- ○

THIS WEEK I FELT

NEXT WEEK I WANT TO

MOST REWARDING INTERACTION I HAD THIS WEEK

THINGS I ACCOMPLISHED THIS WEEK

WHAT WAS THE BEST THING ABOUT THE WEEK?

MY RANKING OF THE WEEK

☆ ☆ ☆ ☆ ☆

People / Places / Experience that filled your heart with love and joy in the last few weeks

Pour your heart out

Pour your heart out

Pour your heart out

Pour your heart out

Pour your heart out

Pour your heart out

The best way to end anything is with

gratitude

www.ingramcontent.com/pod-product-compliance
Lightning Source LLC
LaVergne TN
LVHW021142160826
845679LV00023B/2005